CORNWALL COUNTY LIBRARY

3 8009 0107

GW01336291

/620.00924 BRU

5 DEC 1992

- 4 MAR 2006

WITHDRAWN

ADAMS, J.
Isambard
Kingdom
Brunel
0711703000
C/620.00924 BRU

NF

ZL

ADAMS, J.
Isambard Kingdom Brunel
0711703000

WITHDRAWN

CORNWALL COUNTY COUNCIL
LIBRARIES AND ARTS DEPARTMENT

ONE AND ALL

inside it using picks and shovels to
el face. Bricklayers followed the shield
apidly as they could, lined the newly
ole with cement and bricks to prevent
g. The idea was derived from Marc
he marine worm *Teredo navalis* which
damage to wooden ships by chewing
gh the timbers of the hull creating
ined with its own excrement. Without
mes Tunnel and many similar ventures
been completed. Even so, this pioneer
t was fraught with danger, brought
to bankruptcy and nearly killed young

. Knox, dated 27 March 1876 and titled
eading. It shows a Great Western Railway
past Reading on the 'up' line which, as
still understands today, means towards
London use the 'down' line. Surprisingly
curate pictures of railway trains were
times; this depicts a Rover class broad-
t in the 1870s, running with what is
xperimental design of cab of a different
o these engines in later years. All broad-
nally removed from the Great Western

nd Art Gallery

Isambard who was, at the age of twenty-one, resident engineer in charge of the construction.

The tunnel was being driven through very treacherous ground and the Thames was little better than an open sewer whose poisonous waters brought death and disease to the tunnellers. Isambard displayed great courage, energy, powers of leadership and stamina that set him apart even by the hard standards of the time. The Tunnel Company's directors made an almost impossible task even more difficult by insisting that the public should be allowed to see the workings and arranging frequent visits by the notability of the day. Forty workmen and powerful steam-pumps were required to keep the tunnel clear of floodwater. On 8 May 1827 the tunnellers broke into a large hole in the river-bed left by gravel-dredgers and the tunnel was completely flooded. Nearly 20,000 cubic feet of clay were required to close the breach and it was several months before the tunnel could be pumped dry enough for excavations to start again.

By Saturday, 10 November in the same year, Brunel was proclaiming his confidence by holding a banquet beneath the Thames. Under brilliant gas-lighting, fifty guests and 120 miners – in separate arches of the tunnel – ate their food, were entertained by the band of the Coldstream Guards and toasted Admiral Codrington, one of the tunnel's promoters, when his victory over the Turkish fleet at Navarino was announced.

Just over two months later, all thought of celebration was swept away by another great incursion of water. This time four men were killed and Isambard was seriously injured, escaping death by drowning by the narrowest of margins. While he was recovering, work on the tunnel was abandoned and was not to be resumed until 1836. Finally, in 1843, eighteen years after it was begun, the tunnel was officially opened. Meanwhile, what prospects were open to a young, ambitious, but injured engineer?

An illustration of the Thames Tunnel published in 1851 when the Great Exhibition was staged at the Crystal Palace in Hyde Park. The tunnel was opened in 1843 but only to pedestrians; Marc Brunel's original plans for spiral ramps to enable horse-drawn vehicles to use it were never completed owing to shortage of money. The tunnel served no practical commercial purpose, therefore, until it was adapted in 1865 to serve as a railway tunnel. It remains in use as the most easterly link across the Thames on London's railway network.

Guildhall Library, London

OPPORTUNITIES IN BRISTOL

Established by events after 1828, the link between Bristol, the premier city of the west of England, and the career of one of the nineteenth century's most controversial professional engineers was as accidental as it was productive. During a long period of convalescence, Isambard Brunel had much time to think about the future of his career and although he never doubted his own potential for achieving great things, he was well aware that circumstances beyond his control might doom him to mediocrity. The Stephensons, another father and son partnership, were busily engaged on the country's leading steam railway enterprise, the Liverpool to Manchester railway; Telford had finished the mail-coach road to Holyhead in north Wales, crowning it in 1826 with the great iron suspension bridge across the Menai Straits between the mainland and Anglesey; but for Brunel there was no successfully completed work that would identify him as *the* rising engineer of the day.

The Brunels' tunnel had met with disaster, or so it must have seemed to them at the time, and Marc Brunel's failing health and fortune were further reasons for Isambard to set his own course. With typical Brunelian perseverance, they had invested much time and effort in trying to harness one of Faraday's discoveries about liquified gas, to build a carbonic acid gas engine – a *gaz* machine – that would employ the huge expansive force derived from heating liquified gas. After exposing themselves and their assistant to considerable danger, they eventually had to admit defeat; another blow for the family team.

Brunel made important improvements to entrances and the means of dredging Bristol's Floating Harbour, which was the local name given to the non-tidal dock system created by a famous engineer of an earlier generation, William Jessop. Jessop's entrance locks, completed in 1809, proved to be too narrow – hence Brunel's problems in getting the *Great Britain* out in 1844. The south entrance lock, on the right, was rebuilt by 1848 to Brunel's much improved design and fitted with unique iron caisson gates in place of the old-style wooden gates, which can be seen on the left-hand (north) lock, which remained unaltered until it was closed altogether in 1873. The iron swing-bridges across the locks were also to Brunel's design; they remain, although not in use, and are now the oldest surviving examples of Brunel's pattern of wrought-iron tubular girder construction.
Bristol City Museum and Art Gallery

The young Brunel was not one to stay in a despondent mood for long, but he did commit his day-dreams to paper, building, as he put it, castles in Spain. He would erect a new London Bridge; engineer tunnels at Gravesend and Liverpool; construct a fleet of ships to storm Algiers; and commission his own grand house which he had already designed and drawn. Brunel did not day-dream for long but set about obtaining commissions for work by travelling with a speed and facility which is impressive even by modern standards, since this was some twenty-five years before the country's main-line railway network had been established.

During the next four years he obtained commissions for drainage works in Essex, the design and construction of an observatory at Kensington for Mr (later Sir) James South and for major dock schemes in Sunderland and Bristol. However, it was another project, which Brunel heard about almost casually from a friend, that forged the link between him and Bristol; this was the contruction of a bridge to span the Avon Gorge at Clifton. It was so important in its own right and as a gateway to future achievements for Brunel that he was moved to write about it later as 'My first child, my darling'.

The proposal to build such a bridge was the result of a legacy of £1,000 which a wealthy Bristol wine merchant, William Vick, had left in trust when he died in 1754. His idea was that his bequest should be invested until £10,000 had been accumulated and that it should then be used to build a stone bridge across the gorge. There was a considerable amount of shipping on the River Avon, travelling from the sea through the gorge and on to the port of Bristol some three-quarters of a mile further upstream and, as even a modest cargo vessel required about 100 feet of clearance for its masts at high water, any stone bridge would have needed to be a very high and massive affair.

In fact it was not feasible to build a bridge entirely of stone at Clifton. The impracticality was demonstrated in the only design for a stone bridge published by the appropriately named William Bridges in 1793. His design had so much accommodation it would have resembled a small town, complete with a museum! In any case, by the mid-1820s, Telford's magnificent suspension bridge across the Menai Straits had clearly demonstrated that the science of bridge-building had advanced rapidly in the early nineteenth century. Iron, the material of the Industrial Revolution, made a bridge that could span Bristol's gorge a possibility. A bridge committee was

This shows what remains today of the old, south entrance – Brunel's lock – which once connected the tidal River Avon with Bristol's non-tidal Floating Harbour. The iron caisson gates fitted into deep recesses in the lock wall to allow the maximum clearance for vessels. The carefully profiled walls and floor also enabled heavily laden vessels with a greater draught than before to use the lock. It served the port of Bristol well for many years during the mid-nineteenth century but became obsolete when a new, larger entrance lock was completed in 1873; the gates were removed in 1906 and the lock was sealed off.
Bristol City Museum and Art Gallery

formed and in 1829 it announced a competition to find a suitable design for an *iron* bridge.

The result was far from straightforward and the problems arising from the competition took two years to resolve. From the beginning, Brunel was determined to win the commission but found his designs being rejected not once but twice. In the second design competition he was placed second, but obtained an appointment with the judges, quickly dealt with the technical matters that had influenced the placings and overwhelmed them with enthusiasm for his 'Egyptian thing' – the latest set of designs he had produced for a suspension bridge with supporting towers decorated with sphinxes and cast-iron panels in the style of an Egyptian temple, telling the story of the bridge's construction. The judges changed their minds, declared Isambard Brunel the winner and three months later work began, on 21 June 1831.

Brunel was never to see the Clifton Bridge completed.

The design for a suspension bridge across the River Avon at Clifton, decorated in the style of an Egyptian temple, which Brunel persuaded the judges of the second Clifton Bridge competition to accept in 1830. The fine pen-and-ink drawing of the bridge structure is by Brunel, although the background is believed to have been added by a noted Bristol artist of the time, Samuel Jackson.

Bristol City Museum and Art Gallery

Serious riots later in the year, caused by popular agitation for Parliamentary reforms, left the civic and commercial leaders of Bristol wary and lacking in confidence and work on the bridge stopped. A fresh start was made in 1836, but by then Brunel was busy with his next major project, the construction of a railway line between Bristol and London. Genuine constructional difficulties with the massive bridge abutments and lack of money caused the project to be halted again in 1843. Many people, including Brunel, thought the idea had been abandoned for ever; others called for the demolition of the towers which stood strong, but useless, above the gorge.

Brunel died in 1859; a year later, a new company was formed by leading members of the Institution of Civil Engineers who were determined to finish the Clifton Bridge as a monument to one of their founding and most highly regarded members, to remove 'a slur from the engineering talent of the country'. Brunel's friend and steadfast supporter, Captain Christopher Claxton, became secretary of the company, which went to great expense to obtain a new Act of Parliament authorising completion of the bridge and empowering its trustees to charge tolls to pay for and then maintain it.

Work resumed in 1862 with a confidence that was, at last, justified. One remaining obstacle, the provision of suitable suspension chains, was solved by a curious turn of events. Brunel had 'condescended to engineer' a pedestrian bridge which enabled the residents of south London to reach an enclosed market hall at Hungerford on the north bank of the River Thames. Completed in 1843, the bridge was, as perhaps may be expected, similar in many details to the then partially completed Clifton Bridge. Hungerford Market was bought by the South Eastern Railway Company for the Charing Cross terminus which still occupies the site today; Brunel's footbridge was dismantled in 1862, its chains refurbished and then placed across the Avon Gorge in Bristol in 1863, resting on the towers designed more than thirty years before.

By 1864, it was possible to walk across the gorge on a bridge, not of stone as William Vick had envisaged but of iron. The main supporting elements, its towers, the abutments and the chains had all been made while Brunel was alive; only the roadway girders, decking and suspension rods were new, but even their design was little altered from Brunel's concept. Today the Clifton Bridge carries far more traffic than could ever have been envisaged in Brunel's time; over four million vehicles crossed it in 1973 before a new motorway bridge across the Avon was completed. It remains in daily use, a joy to see and a spectacular monument to its designer.

THE GREAT WESTERN RAILWAY

Even before it was finished, the railway Brunel designed between London and Bristol was exciting passions. The first approaches to Parliament were limited because of shortages of shareholders' capital and so it was proposed to start constructing the ends of the line first, at Bristol and London, before commencing the connecting section between Bath and Reading. This was dismissed as 'neither *Great*, nor *Western* nor even a *Railway* at all'. In later years, the railway's initials, GWR, were designated 'God's Wonderful Railway' or the 'Great Way Round' depending upon viewpoint.

In the rivalry between Bristol and Liverpool for trans-Atlantic trade, Bristol's docks were becoming less attractive to ship-owners. Improvements were made over the years but generally characterised as too little and too late. By 1830, the Stephensons' railway from Liverpool had reached Manchester, and Bristol merchants were afraid that the northern port would draw even further ahead by being first with a rail link to London. So in 1832, meetings were held between representatives of influential Bristol groups with the idea of establishing a railway to London; funds for a preliminary survey and an engineer's report were raised.

Brunel was one of several candidates anxious to undertake the work, but he flatly refused to take part in any contest in which the contract would go automatically to the engineer submitting the lowest price for the project. The railway committee evidently approved of this 'nothing-but-the-best' attitude and appointed the twenty-seven-year-old Brunel to be their engineer in March 1833. W. H. Townsend was also appointed as

The Clifton Suspension Bridge in 1863, during the final phase of construction. Two sets of iron wires passed over the towers were used to support a wooden staging, upon which the forged-iron links of the suspension chains were assembled, working from the ground anchorages on either side, towards the centre. The girders forming the road-deck were then fastened to vertical suspension rods, attached to the chains.
Bristol City Museum and Art Gallery

Brunel's Clifton Bridge is, today, almost as he designed it in 1830, except for the elaborate Egyptian-style decorations which were never made because they proved too expensive. A popular tourist attraction and on a busy commuter route into the city, the bridge carries more traffic than its designer could have imagined and will continue to remain in use well into the twenty-first century.

Austin J. Brown Aerial Photography, Bristol

Brunel's assistant and together they were to make a survey of the line for £500 in less than three months. Covering every inch of the ground on foot or on horseback Brunel was to earn his nickname – the Little Giant. Working twenty hours a day seeking the best route and when it was too dark to see, working indoors on plans and reports, even Brunel admitted that the work 'was harder than I liked'. Nevertheless his report was ready in time and the newly formed company quickly applied to Parliament for permission to raise capital and build the railway.

Many early railway lines were fiercely opposed in Parliament by landowners and others who objected to the notion of a public transport system encroaching on their privacy, or, as in the case of the operators of the country's canal system and horse-drawn road-coaches, the threat to their livelihood. Brunel gave breathtaking performances as a technical witness at the many committee hearings and public meetings which attended the passage of the GWR Bill through Parliament and proved to be an accomplished diplomat when dealing with hostile landowners. The first application to Parliament was rejected in 1834, but the second Bill received Royal Assent on 31 August 1835.

Brunel astutely observed that the Parliamentary Act approving another railway line did not stipulate the gauge of the track that was to be used so he arranged for a similar omission from the GWR Bill of 1835. He became convinced that a broader gauge of seven feet would be preferable to the four-foot-eight-and-a-half-inch gauge then commonly used by the Stephensons and other contemporary railway engineers. Higher speed and greater comfort were what Brunel promised the Great Western's directors and shareholders and although this was partly achieved, it proved to be the greatest single error of judgment Brunel was to make in his career. Parliament decided in 1845 to adopt four feet, eight and a half inches as the gauge for any new major public railway which meant Brunel's Great Western lines were immediately non-standard compared with most of the country's railways. He was perhaps too busy to realise that instead of his superior broad-gauge line setting the nation's standard and other railways being forced to change to suit, *his* railway system would eventually be the one that would have to be altered at vast cost.

It was of course an enormous task for one man to direct and inspire an entire railway undertaking on this scale; Brunel and many of his contemporaries, such as Robert Stephenson, were to pay a dear price in health and eventually with their lives for the physical and mental strain of the work they did in the 1830s and 40s. And if the engineers directing the project suffered, so too did the men and horses whose muscle-power was used to build the line. There were few mechanical aids and the *navvies* (so named after the previous generation of canal *navigation* builders) prided themselves on their ability to shift fourteen tons of 'muck' every day they worked, using only a pick and shovel.

Construction began at both ends of the line with resident assistant engineers in Bristol and London working to Brunel's instructions. Brunel attempted to be everywhere, travelling in the *Flying Hearse* – his black carriage adapted with plan storage, a sleeping bunk and a drawing board. The Bristol end of the line required the greatest amount of civil engineering work and the local committee of directors provided sufficient funds to allow Brunel to demonstrate his flair for architectural embellishment and grand designs.

The first section of the Great Western Railway that opened to the public ran from a temporary terminus at Paddington in London to Taplow near Maidenhead on 4 June 1838. The railway's directors and guests had celebrated the event a few days before with a lunch and 'the usual complement of toasts'; their journey back to London was enlivened as Thomas Guppy, one of the founder directors, walked on the carriage roofs as the train proceeded on its way! Unfortunately the public was less enthusiastic about the railway and its services. The locomotives Brunel had ordered from various manufacturers proved unreliable and the carriages of the time were so badly designed and sprung that the ride was harsh. However, Brunel's gift for nearly always choosing the right associates overcame many of the early troubles and set the railway on course for successful growth.

Daniel Gooch was appointed by Brunel to be the line's Superintendent of Locomotives in 1837; although only in his early twenties, he was an experienced locomotive engineer who had learnt his trade with the Stephensons in Newcastle. He quickly designed new engines to replace the mediocre assortment that had been built in 1837 by different firms to Brunel's specifications and which proved so embarrassingly inadequate when the railway began to run trains in 1838. While the new Firefly class locomotives were being built, Brunel and Gooch had to make do with what engines they had and even spent Christmas Day in 1838 in the workshops improving the blast-pipe of an engine to make it work better. Gooch's work saved Brunel's reputation and stemmed the tide of criticism which looked at one point as if it might force the railway's directors to seek Brunel's resignation as engineer. The men became lifelong friends and Daniel Gooch went on to become Chairman of the Great Western Railway in 1865, a post he held for twenty-four years.

Although competent assistants and contractors were able to play their part, numerous problems to do with the line's construction were referred to Brunel in person. Many structures on the line still in use today can truthfully be said to be the product of his ingenious mind. His delight in seeking elegant solutions to seemingly insurmountable problems confounded many critics who

The controversial tunnel at Box remains in daily use by modern trains, its ornamental façades little altered from when they were first built. This is the portal of the western (lower) end of the tunnel. Brunel has perhaps received more than his fair share of criticism because he had exaggerated the proportions of such features far more than was strictly required in functional terms, even allowing for the greater scale of his broad-gauge line. However, he regarded the railway as 'the finest work in England' and therefore deserving of grand architecture such as this.
Bristol City Museum and Art Gallery

found his style of engineering hard to accept. His bridge across the Thames at Maidenhead is a classic example of his ability to work with style and a sense of fun at a time when other men would have been brought low by the pressure of work and responsibility.

The line crossed the Thames at Maidenhead barely twenty-five feet above the river, which is 290 feet wide at this point; the navigation channel and tow path had to be kept clear and the bridge structure had to allow floodwater to escape. Brunel took all these factors into account, designing a bridge with two of the longest and flattest unsupported brick arches ever built, each arch spanning 128 feet but rising only twenty-four feet six inches to the centre. Many people were convinced such flat arches could not stand and were cynically delighted when some of the supporting timberwork was taken down by the building contractor and one arch distorted; it was admitted by the contractor that it was his fault because the cement was not properly set and he rectified the damage at his own expense. The timber supporting the other main arch was left in place, or so the critics thought. Brunel had had the crucial timbers removed once the cement on this arch was dry and it remained standing soundly, as it does today; he left what appeared to be supporting timber in place until nature abetted Brunel's confidence trick and blew it down, dumbfounding critics who had been predicting for over a year that the bridge could not stand without support.

Two other major pieces of engineering out of the many on the 110-mile-long line between London and Bristol deserve to be mentioned; Sonning Cutting in Berkshire and Box Tunnel, where the line travelling westwards begins to descend towards Bath. Both undertakings illustrate the problems facing the pioneer railway engineers, because the scale of the work they were doing was far greater than many contractors who tendered for work on the line realised. Indeed some problems were harder to solve than even Brunel or his most competent assistants could anticipate. Contractors often undertook to do work which was beyond their capacity and this delayed the construction and cost the railway company dearly by forcing them to pay for some work twice. Such was the case at Sonning, where William Ranger got hopelessly behind with his contract to excavate a cutting nearly two miles long and sixty feet deep in places.

Brunel had originally intended tunnelling through the obstructions at Sonning but later chose an open cutting; Ranger was dismissed from this and another contract nearer Bristol. He sought compensation from the company in a famously protracted case that was not settled for nearly twenty years. Even when the Sonning work was divided up between three contractors, the

Most of Britain's main railway lines were completed before it was possible to photograph them under construction. However, this lithograph by John Bourne, published in 1837, showing dozens of horse-drawn 'barrow-runs' in Tring Cutting on Robert Stephenson's London and Birmingham line, gives a fascinating glimpse of just one of the methods used by engineers of Brunel's time for removing soil and stone from deep cuttings.

Bristol City Museum and Art Gallery

The famous bridge across the River Thames at Maidenhead remains in daily use over 150 years after Brunel's critics had so confidently predicted that its low elliptical arches would collapse. The main line between Taplow and Didcot was doubled to four tracks in 1890–92, but the original bridge was not touched; a second, separate bridge faithfully replicating Brunel's design was constructed alongside, so that no visible change occurred. This was, in itself, a great tribute to Brunel's skill as a bridge designer.

failure of one of them eventually forced Brunel to take personal charge. He brought a sense of urgency to the work and in 1839 between 20,000 and 30,000 cubic yards of earth were regularly being removed every week. A main road was carried across the cutting by another of Brunel's brick arched bridges and a minor road used a wooden bridge in a style that was to become familiar on the lines, particularly in Cornwall, that eventually continued the route to Penzance.

Brunel always regarded the Box Tunnel near Bath as the most important work on the railway and was emphasising to the directors in 1836 that it 'will determine the completion of the line'. Nearly two miles long and inclined on a gradient of 1 in 100, it was the most ambitious railway tunnel so far attempted and provoked almost hysterical responses from many people, including other engineers. However, one of Brunel's best personal assistants, William Glennie, remained resident engineer in charge throughout the six years the tunnel took to build. Three contractors built the tunnel. George Burge of Herne Bay excavated over three-quarters of its length through clay, blue marl and inferior oolite, which had to be lined with over thirty million bricks made by Hunt of Chippenham. The other two contractors, Lewis of Bath and Brewer of Box made superhuman efforts to blast through half a mile of Bath stone; theirs proved to be the most difficult task, as water flooded into the tunnel at such a rate during the winter of 1837 that it overwhelmed the steam-pumps and rose fifty-six feet up the access shafts.

For two and a half years a ton each of gunpowder and candles were used every week; after August 1840, when the tunnel was threatening to delay the opening of the line which everywhere else was nearing completion, 4,000 men and 300 horses worked day and night. By the time it was finished in June 1841, two months before the line was opened throughout, over 100 men had been killed working to finish what had been dismissed as that

A modern oil painting by Terence Cuneo recreates the thrilling sight of one of Daniel Gooch's Firefly engines emerging from Box Tunnel on its way to Bath and Bristol. As no original broad-gauge locomotives have been preserved, the *Firefly Trust* was set up in Bristol in 1981 to build accurate working replicas of a Firefly engine and some early broad-gauge Great Western carriages. Scheduled for completion in 1990, the Firefly train will carry passengers on lengths of specially laid broad-gauge track in Bristol and other places associated with the early GWR.
Firefly Trust

John Bourne's lithograph of Sonning Cutting, on the Great Western Railway, was published in 1846. The tressel bridge, carrying the road from Sonning to Loddon Bridge over the railway, is an early example of this type of low-cost structure, made of Baltic yellow pine, which Brunel used extensively on the Cornwall Railway. The other bridge carrying the Great Western turnpike road (the modern A4 route), was a more conventional and costly red brick and stone structure.

Bristol City Museum and Art Gallery

'monstrous and extraordinary, most dangerous and impracticable tunnel at Box'.

Even when the work was done, Brunel was not to be left in peace. In 1842, an eminent geologist, who had not actually been inside the tunnel, claimed that the section excavated through the Bath stone which had been left unlined was unsafe. Three years later after severe frost had caused a minor rock-fall from one of the airshafts, the same geologist was persuaded to visit the tunnel and declared himself convinced of its safety.

The construction of a station at Slough had been opposed by the Masters of Eton College who, on the pretext that the line would have a bad influence on the morals of the pupils, ensured that the GWR Bill precluded the construction of a station within three miles of the college. However, they relented after the railway laid on a special train to take the boys to London for the Coronation of Queen Victoria in 1837. Slough Station opened in June 1840. Queen Victoria became the first British monarch to travel by train when she journeyed from Slough Station to London in June 1842. This station, together with the one at Reading, had been designed by Brunel with both the up and down platforms on the same side of the line, which

Facing page: The interior of the building that Brunel designed as the Bristol terminus for the Great Western Railway has survived to the present day remarkably unchanged; it is now regarded as the prime example of a main-line railway station built during the railway age of the 1830s and 40s. The lithograph by J. C. Bourne, published in 1846, depicts one of Daniel Gooch's Firefly class engines ready to depart with a London-bound train. The modern photograph shows how little the structure has changed. It was used as a railway station until 1966 and is currently being renovated by the Brunel Engineering Centre Trust as a science centre, a civil-engineering museum and a working centre for local conservation and environmental groups. Parts of the building, including some of the offices used by the Bristol-based board of directors of the GWR, are open to the public.
Bristol City Museum and Art Gallery

Below: The train shed Brunel designed as the Bristol terminus of the GWR may be seen to the right of this photograph, taken in about 1870, shortly before the building was extended to form part of a new station complex. Mixed gauge track was laid into the station in 1855 by the Midland Railway Company. Until 1872, the Bristol and Exeter Railway used a separate terminus consisting of the mundane wooden station building (left) and the grandiose stone office building (centre).
Bristol City Museum and Art Gallery

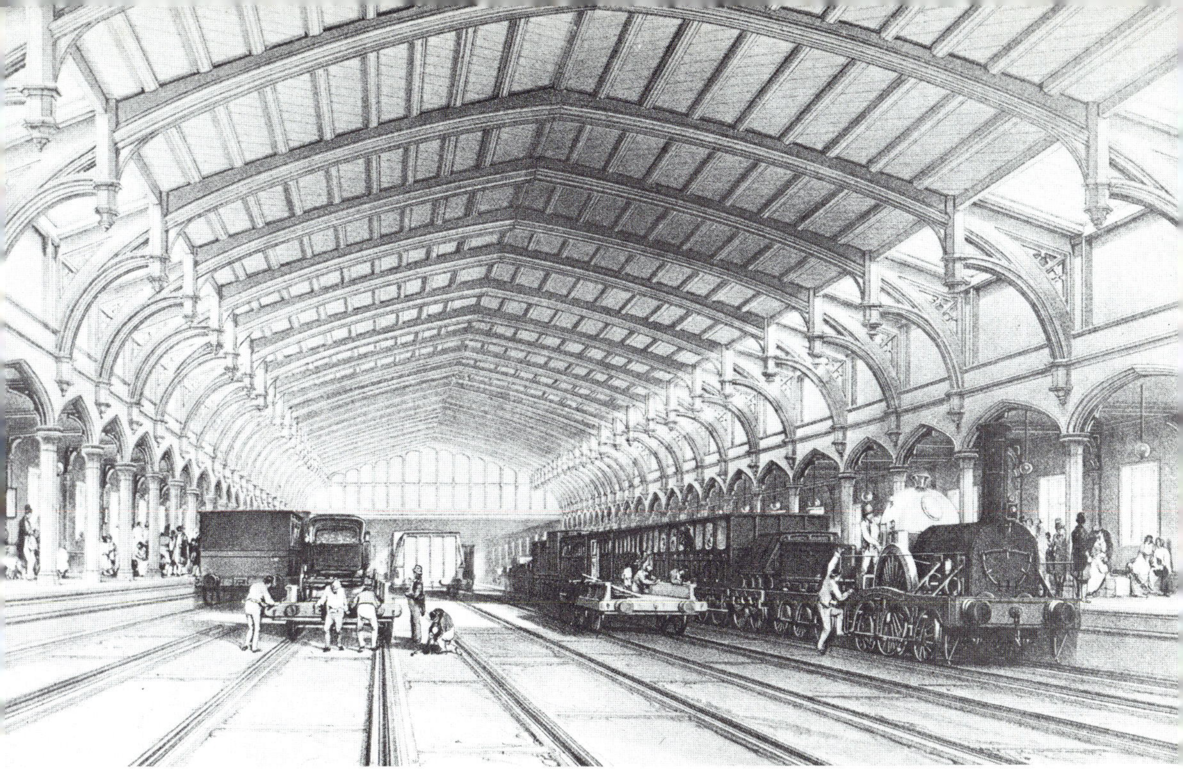

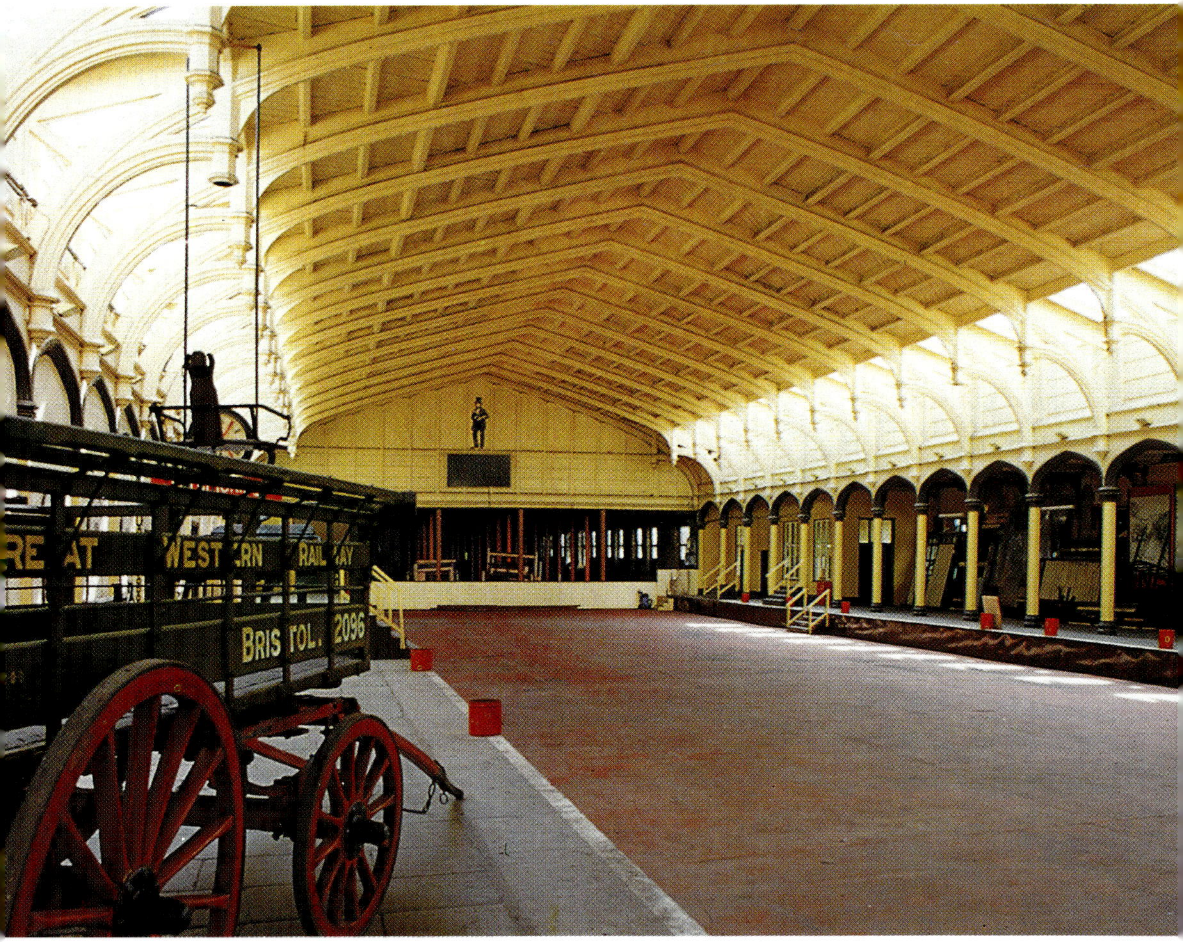
WESTERN
BRISTOL. 2096

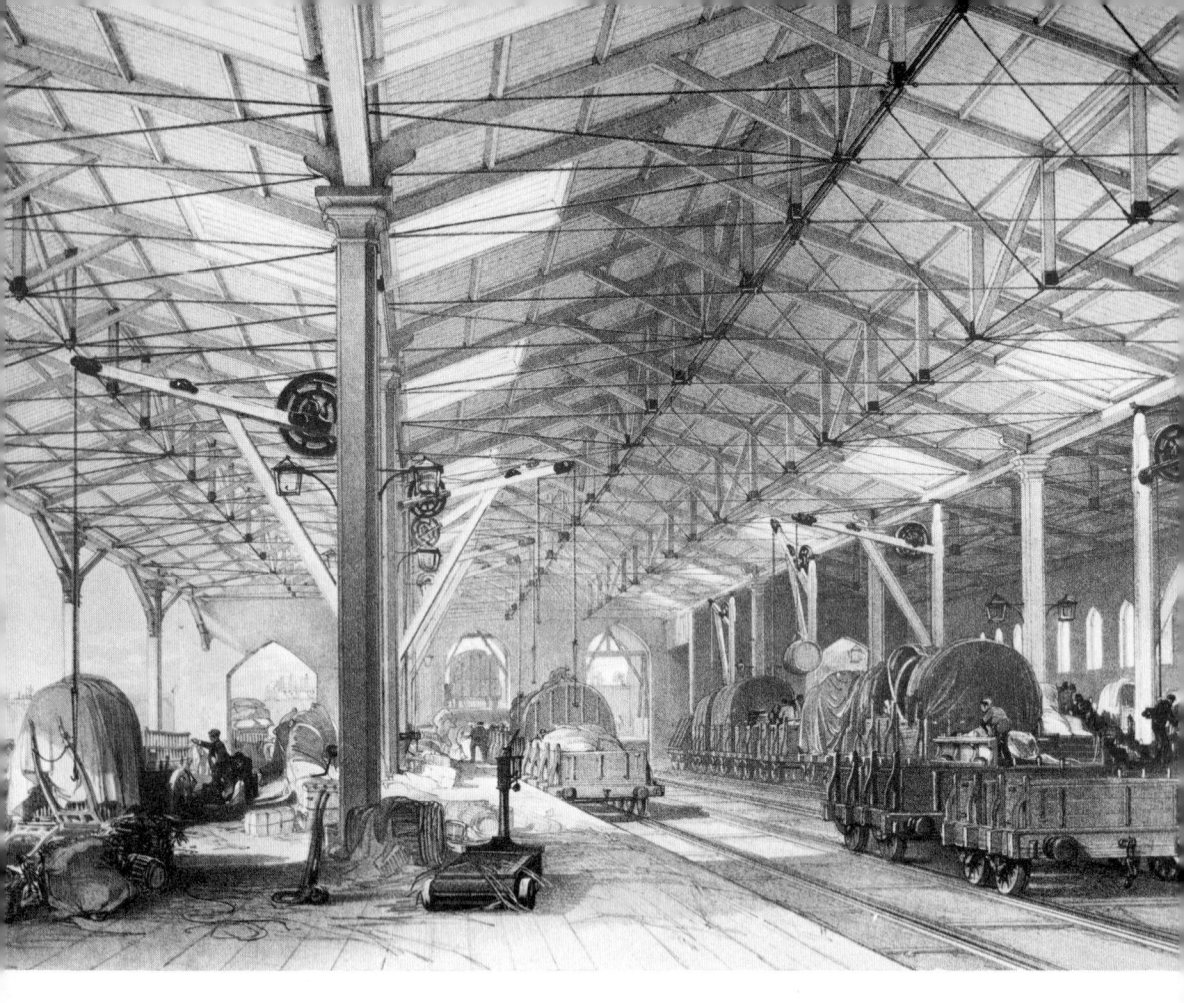

The passenger terminus at Bristol was built on brick arches some fifteen feet above the road level at which the goods shed was situated. Therefore, goods wagons had to be moved from the main line above, first by rotating them on turntables and then lowering them into the shed on hydraulically powered lifts, capable of lifting 10-ton loads in about half a minute.

Bristol City Museum and Art Gallery

necessitated trains travelling in opposite directions to cross in front of one another, a potentially lethal arrangement, but one which Brunel must have felt (in these early days of rail travel) helped passengers by avoiding the need to cross to opposite platforms or the danger of being whisked off in a different direction to the one intended. Several other Great Western stations were also laid out in this idiosyncratic style, but the Board of Trade, the regulating body for railway safety, soon had them all changed to the conventional pattern.

Many sections of the western end of the line were delayed by constructional difficulties of one sort or another, but on 31 August 1840, a little over two years after the first passengers had travelled between London and Taplow, the first train to carry fare-paying passengers from the barely finished terminus at Temple Meads in Bristol was pulled on its way by one of Gooch's Firefly class locomotives, named *Arrow*. This engine was the product of a newly established Bristol firm of locomotive engineers trading with the somewhat unprepossessing name of Stothert and Slaughter. It arrived with its train of excited passengers thirty-three minutes later at an even less ready station at Bath. Ten trains eventually carried 5,880 passengers between Bristol and Bath that day earning £476 for the company. A year later the Great Western Railway was finished and work was already in progress on the Bristol and Exeter line and the South Devon Railway that were to take the railway age, and Brunel's broad-gauge lines, through the heart of south-west England.

Passengers travelling by train to South Wales and the west of England from London will commence their journey in this station at Paddington, which Brunel designed in association with Digby Wyatt, the secretary of the Executive Committee of the Great Exhibition which was responsible for the Crystal Palace. The Great Western Railway was originally intended to share a terminus building at Euston with the London and Birmingham Railway; however, for seventeen years the Great Western used a temporary terminus at Bishop Road, half a mile west of the present station, which was opened in 1854.

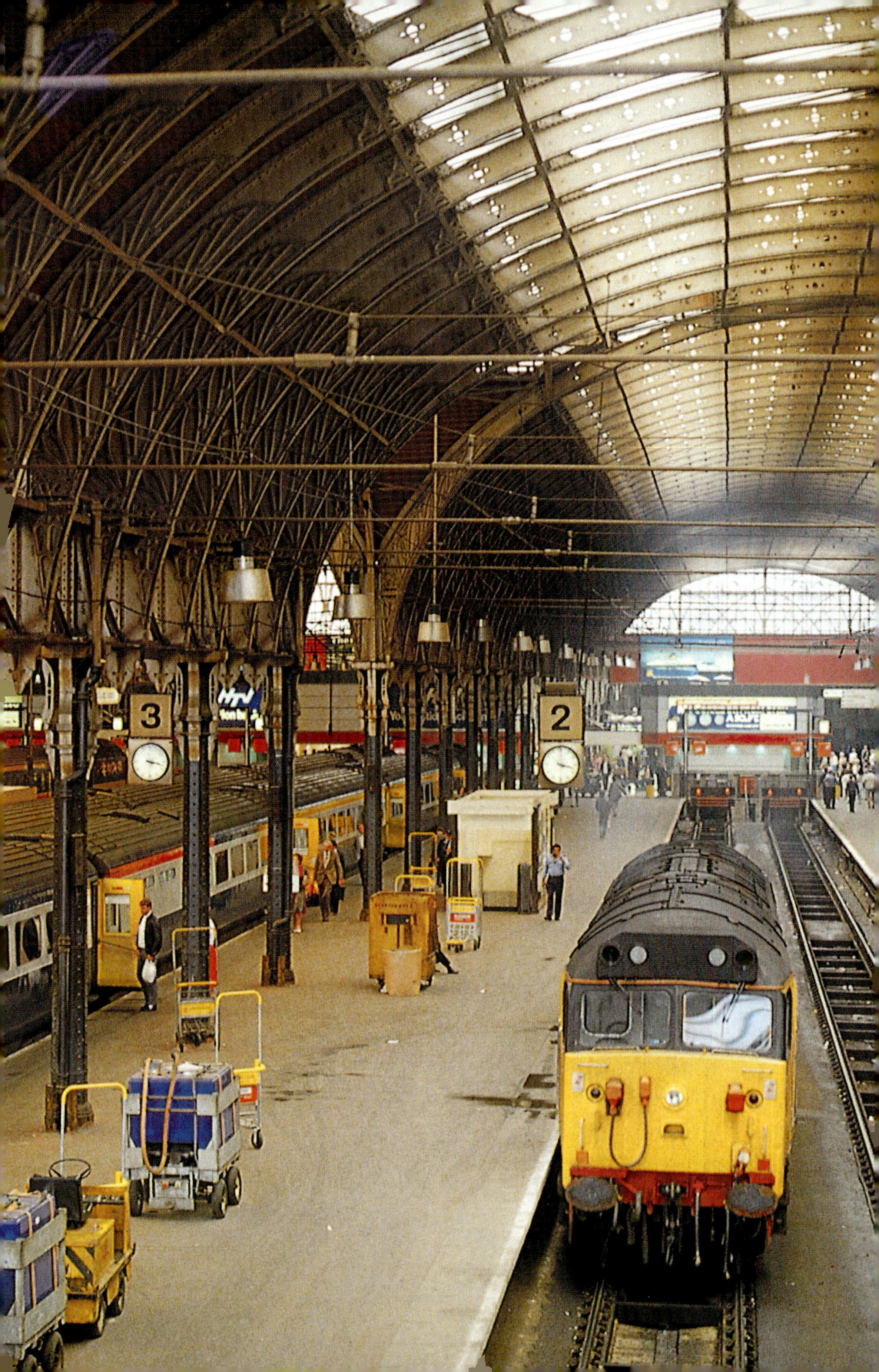
3
2

THE BRISTOL SHIPS

Planned to link directly with the Great Western Railway at Bristol, the creation of a trans-Atlantic steamship service to New York added another vast and startling dimension to Brunel's already dramatic career. At an early board meeting, the railway's directors voiced serious misgivings about the enormous length of the proposed main line to Bristol. Such timidity was almost certain to draw a response from Brunel who retorted: 'Why not make it longer, and have a steamboat go from Bristol to New York and call it the *Great Western*.' However, Thomas Guppy, a trained engineer and owner of a Bristol sugar refinery, took Brunel's remark seriously and the Great Western Steamship Company was formed as a separate undertaking from the railway.

At the time, this represented an unprecedented leap into the unknown; many people genuinely believed that a steamship that was large enough to carry sufficient fuel to allow it to cross the Atlantic under its own power could not be built. Dr Dionysius Lardner gave public lectures proving, so he thought, the impossibility of such voyages; even Marc Brunel, who patented several improvements in marine steam engines had said, 'my opinion is that steam cannot do for distant navigation'. However,

This photograph, one of a series taken in November 1857 by Robert Howlett, is the image of Brunel that has been most reproduced and for many characterises the man best; hands shoved into pockets, a lighted cigar in his mouth, the engineering genius ready to face his next challenge. He was however, nearing the end of his life when this picture was taken, fatigued with all the financial and practical worries of trying to finish the *Great Eastern* steamship. He, nevertheless, could still make fun of his circumstances, noting in his diary that he had asked an associate to stand with him beside one of the huge drums of chain, designed to steady the *Great Eastern* during her launch, 'but he would not, so I alone am hung in chains'.

Bristol City Museum and Art Gallery

A watercolour of Bristol's harbour in 1836 records, almost by chance, the wooden hull of the paddle-steamship *Great Western*, nearing completion in William Patterson's shipyard at Wapping (right centre). This and all the other large-scale shipbuilding yards in Bristol have closed and the site of the birthplace of the first trans-Atlantic ocean liner has become the Bristol Industrial Museum, opened in 1978, in a dockside transit shed built in 1952. A plaque commemorating the launch of the *Great Western* may be seen on the end wall of the museum building facing Wapping Road.

Bristol City Museum and Art Gallery

Isambard was once again able to demonstrate his ability to see the flaw in a belief universally held.

Brunel crystallised the theory which held the key to long-distance steam-powered navigation: doubling the capacity of a ship's hull (and thereby making it large enough to carry sufficient coal to allow it to travel further) did not double its surface area. A larger hull needs a bigger engine and more fuel but because the surface area (and therefore the resistance of the hull to being propelled through the water) has not increased by the same amount, the bigger ship actually saves a proportion of its fuel compared to a smaller one and can therefore travel further. Get the proportions of the hull right and steam navigation across the oceans would become a practical proposition.

It was this hard reasoning that turned the dream of trans-Atlantic steamship travel into a reality. Superficially, Brunel's new steamship design was as orthodox as the vessels which had been built in Bristol, London, Liverpool, Glasgow and elsewhere since the 1820s: she would be built of wood, be propelled by paddle-wheels and carry a generous spread of sail. Unlike her contemporaries, however, she would not be limited to coastal and short sea-routes. Her size and strength and the power of her engines would all be greater than that of anything afloat.

Work on the new ship, named *Great Western*, began on 28 July 1836 in the Bristol shipyard of William Patterson on the site now occupied by the Bristol Industrial Museum. On 19 July 1837 she was launched into the widest part of the Bristol harbour. Her engines were being built in London by the firm Maudslay, Sons and Field who had made many of the parts of Marc Brunel's block-making machines and were by now one of the leading manufacturers of steam and marine engines. Less than a month after she was launched, the *Great Western* was sailed to London to have her engines fitted.

After some steaming trials and with her seventy-five-foot-long saloon beautifully decorated and ornamented, the *Great Western* left Blackwall early on 31 March 1838 to return, this time by steam-power, to Bristol to pick up passengers for her maiden voyage. Barely two hours later, the most fearful thing that can happen to a wooden ship occurred: fire. Flames and smoke rose from the forward boiler-room. The captain, Lt James Hosken RN ran the vessel aground off Canvey Island; the chief engineer went below through black smoke, as did the Bristol Harbourmaster, Captain Christopher Claxton RN, who played a hose-pipe on the burning deck-beams.

Brunel fell from a charred ladder into the stoke-hold to lie unconscious face-down in the water accumulating on the boiler-room deck. As he fell, he had knocked Claxton down, but this, and the speed with which Claxton, working in the smoke and darkness, had managed to find him and get him lifted back to the deck, saved his life. Claxton did not discover until after the fire was out that the man who had knocked him down and whose life he had saved was his friend and colleague, Brunel.

Put ashore, Brunel again had to spend some weeks recovering from this, his second narrow escape from death. The *Great Western* meanwhile continued her journey and arrived at Bristol only twelve hours later than planned, on Monday afternoon. Unfortunately, news of the fire had been exaggerated and only seven of the fifty-seven passengers who had paid their fare sailed on the inaugural voyage to America on the following Sunday; not perhaps the most auspicious start to trans-Atlantic steamship travel.

The *Great Western* arrived in New York at 2.00 pm on 23 April, after a fifteen-day voyage from Bristol; bad weather had delayed her sailing and caused some damage at sea and the stokers had proved troublesome. Another steamship, *Sirius*, had beaten *Great Western* by a matter of a few hours to become the first ship to cross the Atlantic using steam engines for the entire journey. Nevertheless, the interest of the huge crowds of spectators who had turned out on this memorable day was centred on Brunel's *Great Western*, because she was clearly the vessel that had been specifically designed for and was capable of operating a genuine trans-Atlantic service. In demonstrating the practical justification of Brunel's theories, she marked a turning-point in maritime history.

The *Great Western* went on to cross the Atlantic for many years with businesslike regularity but, sadly, her Bristol-based owners were not to be rewarded with the commercial success they and her designer so richly deserved. The ship was too big to navigate safely the restricted river approaches to the harbour in Bristol and worked from an anchorage in deeper water near the mouth of the river, as many of the port's larger sailing vessels had been doing since the mid-eighteenth century. Passengers and cargo were transferred to and from Bristol seven miles upstream in tugs and barges. In 1843 the vessel was moved to Liverpool to avoid this inconvenience and expense, although remaining in Bristol ownership until 1847.

A start was made on a second vessel in 1838 but instead of sticking to the same design as the *Great Western*, Brunel's talent for innovation took him, his steamship company and the port of Bristol on a more complicated and less commercially successful course. It was left to a Canadian-born Liverpool ship-owner, Edward Cunard, to exploit the simple commercial option of quickly building several ships like the *Great Western* and thereby securing the lucrative trans-Atlantic mail contract from the British Government, because he could offer a more frequent and regular service than his rivals. Bristolians were not to forgive Brunel when they saw the opportunity of the city's becoming the premier trans-Atlantic steamship port slipping away to Liverpool; although the less favourable location of Bristol and its reluctance to invest the massive sums needed to improve the port were really to blame.

William Patterson (1795–1869), the ship-builder who constructed the *Great Western* and assisted with the design of the *Great Britain*, was born in Arbroath in Scotland. He gained experience of building steamships in the early 1820s, at William Evans' yard in London, before moving to Bristol in 1823. By the time Patterson met Brunel, he had an established reputation for building fast sailing vessels with 'clipper' hulls; the seaworthiness of both of Brunel's Bristol-built steamships must be attributed, in part, to Patterson.
Bristol City Museum and Art Gallery

The *Great Western* made 22 round voyages from Bristol to New York between 8 April 1838 and 6 December 1841. This illustration by the popular Bristol marine painter, J. Walter, depicts the busy, not to say sometimes frenetic, scene which attended the preparations for one of *Great Western*'s voyages from her anchorage at Kingroad in the Bristol Channel. Cargo and passengers had to be ferried from Bristol Harbour some seven miles away in barges and small steamships because the harbour entrance was too small; the vessel was transferred in 1843 to the more convenient Coburg Dock in Liverpool.
Bristol City Museum and Art Gallery

By 1838, Brunel must have been working like a man possessed by demons; his railway lines from London to Bristol and the west of England were at critical stages of construction or design, his pioneer trans-Atlantic steamship was hardly over its teething troubles and he had embarked on the design and construction of another ocean-going steamship, the scale and technology of which was decades ahead of contemporary thinking. It is not surprising perhaps that Brunel either overlooked or simply chose to ignore the more practical and commercial implications of what he was doing in making his second vessel for the Great Western Steamship Company quite unlike anything that had gone before – a huge screw-propelled vessel with an iron hull, named the *Great Britain*. Even the sailing rig fitted to this vessel anticipated by fifty years the design of the last and biggest commercial sailing ships that were built in America and Britain after the 1890s.

Brunel brought the bridge-builder's standards to naval architecture; the hull of the *Great Britain* was considerably longer than that of the *Great Western* which had already exceeded what was then regarded as the safe limits for a wooden hull. An even longer vessel could easily break in two under certain sea conditions, because waves leave large sections of the hull unsupported as they move along its length. Modern naval architects admire the longitudinal girders Brunel designed into the hull of the *Great Britain* and point to them, the watertight bulkheads and the iron decking over the girders in the bottom of the ship, as features which improved the safety record of ships at sea when they were adopted in iron ship construction as standard practice. The fifteen-foot-diameter propeller has been assessed in recent times as of a very efficient design wholly appropriate to the power of the slow-turning steam-engines and, despite a series of not unexpected mechanical problems on early voyages, the *Great Britain* demonstrated that she was a technically more advanced and faster ship than the more conventional paddle-steamer *Great Western*.

The *Great Britain*, however, had taken too long to build and the failure of the impoverished Bristol Dock Company to enlarge the entrance locks to Bristol Harbour at Cumberland Basin further delayed the maiden voyage of the vessel to New York until August 1845, seven years after the *Great Western* had completed hers. The *Great Britain* never sailed as a commercial vessel from Bristol but used Liverpool from the outset as her base. A navigational error sent the ship aground in

The *Great Britain* was built in a dry-dock and so the launching ceremony, advertised throughout Bristol on posters like the one shown (*above right*), consisted of opening the gates of the dock at the moment the Prince Consort broke the customary bottle of wine against the ship's bows. There was great excitement when the ocean-going vessel, then the largest in the world, was towed by a steam-tug from the dock out into the harbour.

Bristol City Museum and Art Gallery

Above: Poster advertising the ballast wharf as the best site from which to view the launch of the *Great Britain*.
Bristol City Museum and Art Gallery

The *Great Britain* remained a popular ship throughout her long and varied career, spent mainly carrying passengers, including many emigrants, from the Port of Liverpool to Australia. Her sailing rig, engines and boilers were altered several times to suit her changing role and this lithograph, based on the painting *Dropping the Pilot* by the Liverpool marine artist S. Walters, shows the *Great Britain* getting under way in 1852 with her, then new, four-mast rig and twin-funnelled boilers. A deckhouse running the entire length of the upper deck had been built so she could carry twice as many passengers as Brunel had originally intended.
Bristol City Museum and Art Gallery

Above: This historic photograph, believed to be the oldest surviving one of a ship, was taken by the British pioneer of photography, William Fox-Talbot, some time in 1844, when the *Great Britain* was moored in Bristol at the Mardyke Wharf on the opposite side of the harbour from where she had been built. The ship was trapped in the harbour because the entrance had not been widened by the Bristol Dock Company as promised during construction. Brunel lost patience and, in December 1844, partially dismantled one of the entrance locks to secure sufficient clearance to get the ship out of Bristol Harbour and away to sea. She never operated commercially from Bristol.
National Maritime Museum

The *Great Britain* was salvaged from the Falkland Islands during the winter of 1969–70 and brought back to Bristol on a steel pontoon, from which she was removed in July 1970 in Bristol's modern docks at Avonmouth. The hull had been repaired so that, with powerful pumps working, it would remain afloat and could be towed up the River Avon and back into the old harbour. This photograph records the historic moment when the vessel passed the dry-dock where she had been built 126 years before.

Paul Elkin

Dundrum Bay off the coast of Ireland on her fifth voyage in September 1846. She had 180 passengers on board, the largest number carried up to that time by any trans-Atlantic steamer. None of the passengers was lost or seriously hurt and the fact that the massive hull, although badly damaged, survived intact enough to be refloated the following year, testified to the strength and safety of such a ship. It was, however, too late to salvage the Great Western Steamship Company, which was driven into liquidation by this accident.

Both of Brunel's Bristol-built ships went on to distinguished commercial careers, although not working on the North American route for which they had been designed. *Great Western* lasted until 1857, sailing between England and the West Indies for the Royal Mail Steam Packet Company. *Great Britain* became established after 1852 for twenty-five years on the route from Liverpool to Melbourne and Sydney in Australia. The engines, boilers, sail-rig and passenger accommodation were altered several times, until by 1857 the vessel had been adapted into what was a conventional sailing ship with auxiliary steam-power. In this guise she was well suited to the Australia run and carried many emigrants to this rapidly developing country. Over 630 passengers were regularly carried on voyages lasting sixty days or more; she remained a popular ship throughout this time and no doubt this in itself is a tribute to her designer, although it is not recorded what Brunel felt about the manner in which his advanced steamship design was altered.

The ultimate fate of the *Great Britain* is in itself one of the most remarkable stories in recent maritime history. After conversion in 1882 into a sailing ship without any engines, sharing the humdrum work assigned to many ageing vessels, of carrying steam-coal from South Wales and returning from America with grain or guano fertiliser, she was so badly damaged in storms off South America that she was abandoned in Port Stanley in the Falkland Islands for use as a coal and wool store. In 1933, an unsuccessful attempt was made to raise funds to preserve Brunel's masterpiece, but four years later, the hull was towed to Sparrow Cove, holed and sunk with the intention of allowing wind and tide to destroy what remained of the vessel. After thirty-three years of these punishing conditions it was clear by the mid-1960s that she was deteriorating rapidly.

By 1969, the *Great Britain Project* had been formed and the funds to salvage the hull and return it to Bristol had been generously provided by an English businessman, Jack Hayward. The rapid development of television broadcasting allowed millions of people to observe the triumphal return of the ship, once more floating on her own keel, beneath the Clifton Bridge and some days later, 127 years to the day, being carefully edged back into the dry-dock in which she had been built, watched by HRH Prince Philip.

The *Great Britain*, now externally almost completely restored to the same rig as when she was first built, is open to the public in Bristol. A full-size working fascimile of her original engines is to be installed.

Paul Elkin

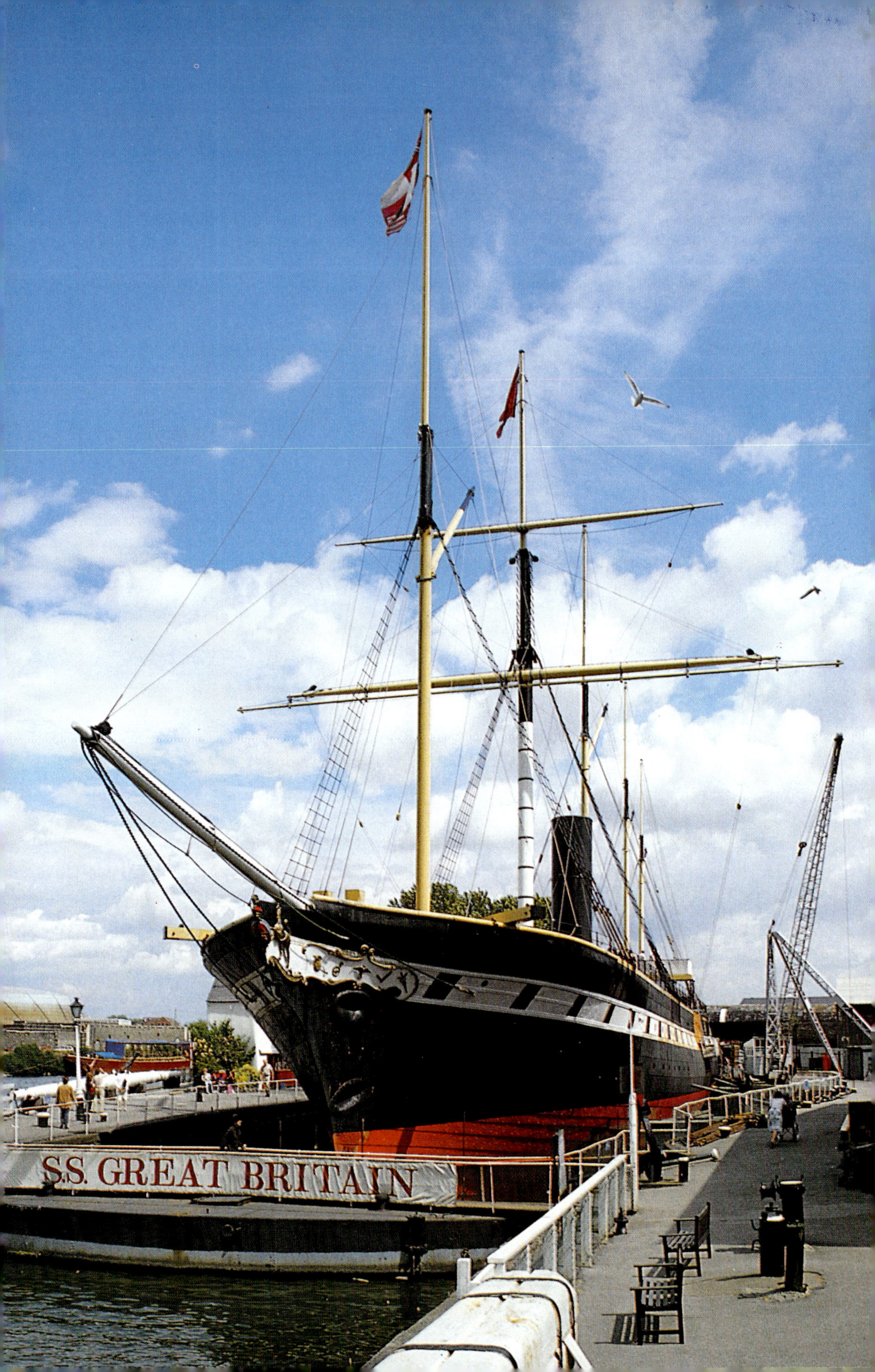
S.S. GREAT BRITAIN

THE ATMOSPHERIC CAPER

There were several occasions during his life when Brunel was the subject of considerable, and often unfair, criticism in the popular press because a project had met with unforeseen difficulties or had cost more than expected. As far as the public was concerned, he made a particularly costly and profligate blunder in 1844 when he recommended an atmospheric propulsion system to power trains on the South Devon Railway. The limited power of early steam railway locomotives forced engineers to create as level a route as they could, often at great cost in civil engineering work. Where there was no alternative but to run a line over a steep gradient, for example on the London and Birmingham Railway between Camden and its London terminus at Euston, trains were pulled up inclines by ropes, driven by steam-winding engines of the type used to haul coal from mines. This arrangement could be used only on relatively straight and short inclines and was no alternative to the steam locomotive for working a long main line.

The attraction, therefore, to railway engineers at this time, of something which resembled an electrically-powered train, capable of travelling almost without noise or fumes, faster and up steeper gradients than any steam train could then manage, and without the restrictions of the cumbersome rope-haulage method must have been very great indeed. The idea of propelling trains using either atmospheric pressure or compressed air had been first proposed in 1810, but a reasonably practical system based on this concept did not appear until 1839, when Samuel Clegg and two brothers, Jacob and Joseph Samuda, combined forces to patent the key feature; a leather flap arranged to act as an air-tight valve running along the top of a continuous iron tube, laid between the rails. Steam-driven pumping stations, positioned at intervals along the track, exhausted air from the tube ahead of a train, which was then pushed forward by atmospheric pressure acting on the back of a piston, attached to a truck, which took the place of a steam locomotive and pulled a train of carriages along. The leather flap valve sealing the tube was lifted momentarily by rollers mounted on the bracket securing the piston to the truck.

Some engineers, including Brunel, Vignoles and Cubitt, were impressed by the system's apparent ability to cope with severe gradients and went on to use it on several stretches of line in Devon, Ireland and at Croydon. Others, including Joseph Locke, shared George Stephenson's view that it was 'a great humbug'. Brunel's proposal to work the fifty-two-mile-long South Devon Railway route between Exeter and Plymouth by the atmospheric system was the most ambitious; the experiment was watched with great interest and some scepticism.

The first route Brunel surveyed in 1836 for a line from Exeter to Plymouth required considerable expenditure on bridges, tunnels and cuttings to avoid any severe gradients on the section south of Dartmoor, between Newton Abbot and Plymouth. It proved too expensive for the South Devon Railway Company and he was compelled therefore to adopt a different route with four inclines longer and steeper than any then planned or being built on a main line railway. In a lengthy report he recommended, in August 1844, that the 'Atmospheric System' be used for running trains over this difficult section of line. It was no spur of the moment decision; in 1840, he had thought about taking trains through the Box Tunnel by atmospheric propulsion and in 1843, had proposed its use through a long tunnel on one of the steep inclines on the Genoa to Turin line for which he was consulting engineer. However, there were many factors which prevented the system from working properly on the South Devon Railway and its failure exposed Brunel to public ridicule.

The line was built during the period in the mid-1840s when speculation in railway construction had been uncontrollable. When this railway mania collapsed, many investors lost money and there followed, in its wake, a period of recrimination and public mistrust which affected engineers like Brunel and Stephenson, despite the fact that they had done their best to disassociate themselves from any scheme they disapproved of in financial as well as engineering terms.

By September 1847, trial operation of atmospheric trains over sections beyond Exeter on the, as yet unfinished, South Devon line, rapidly encountered all manner of difficulties, which often required the passengers to get off and push the carriages. Rats acquired a taste for the seal-oil used to treat the leather flaps, which they ate; what sections were not devoured became stiff and unworkable when exposed to the English climate. In 1848, after less than eight months' operation, Brunel was forced to admit that he had made an error of judgment in recommending the system; it was abandoned and the equipment sold for scrap. A few sections of the cast-iron propulsion tube remain in museums and the pumping station at Starcross, near Exeter, survives as a memorial to Brunel's brave attempt to equip a railway with the latest technology. There can be little doubt that he genuinely believed it would have satisfied the line's motive power requirements effectively and economically.

The South Devon line was completed in April 1849 as a conventional locomotive-hauled railway. Already, significant improvements in steam locomotive design and performance made the working of even such a severely graded route a practical possibility. The 'Atmospheric Caper', as Devonians dubbed it, was over. For Brunel it had been anything but a caper. He suffered great personal anxiety and fatigue and his professional reputation was severely tarnished in the eyes of the public for whom the euphoria of the railway age had gone. Clearly, engineers were not infallible, and errors of judgment on their part could cost a company and its shareholders dearly; Brunel bore the brunt of the criticism directed at his profession.

The only relic of Brunel's atmospheric railway system installed on the South Devon Railway, and open to the public, is this museum housed in the pumping station buildings at Starcross, near Exeter. The steam engines and equipment from Starcross and the other pumping stations that were operated for a time were sold, either for scrap after 1848 or for re-use in mines. The pumping station buildings like this one were used for other purposes; Starcross was a coal depot until the late 1970s.

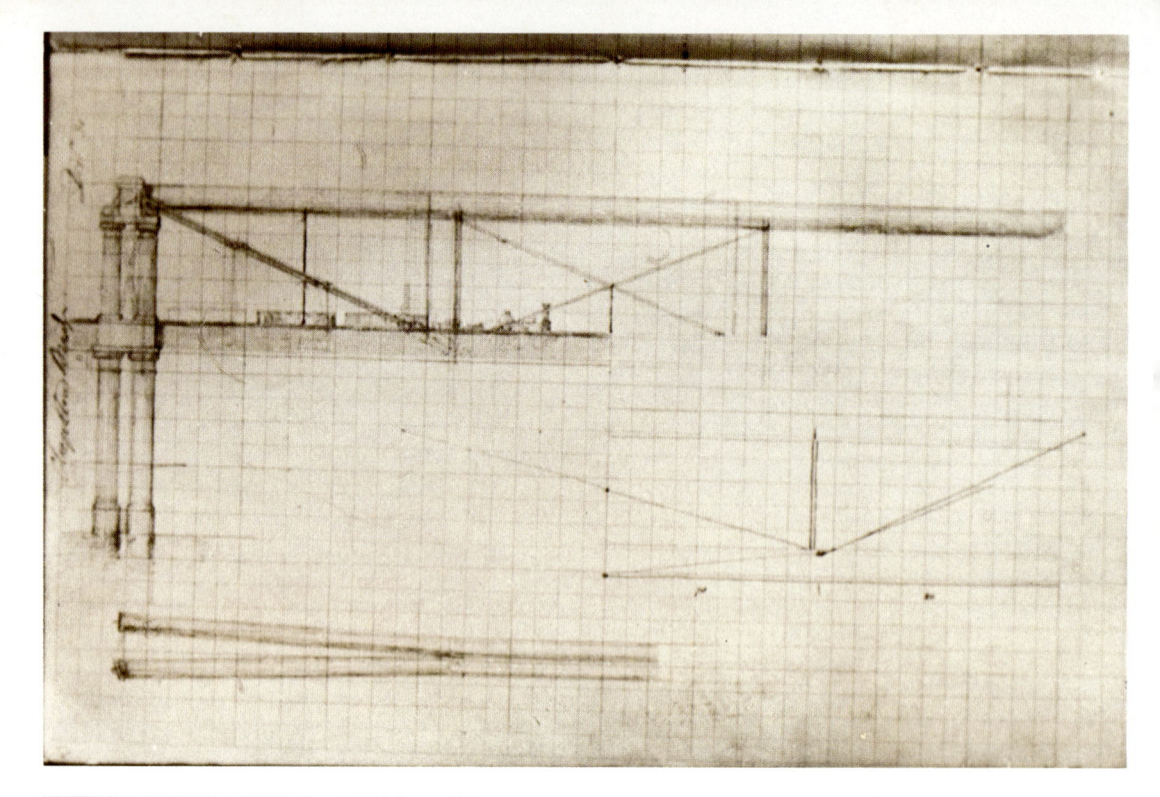

A sketch by I. K. Brunel of the bridge he proposed to build to carry the South Wales Railway across the River Wye at Chepstow. A series of Brunel's notebooks may be seen in the University of Bristol Library by appointment.
University of Bristol

BRUNEL THE BRIDGE-BUILDER

The Clifton Bridge, which established Brunel's career, marks the end of a phase of bridge construction and civil engineering associated with the development of Britain's canal and road system which had gathered considerable momentum after 1775. The great engineers of the early Victorian era turned their attention to railways and, as a direct result of the experience and techniques gained on road and canal work, were able to design some bold structures to carry the railways across the landscape.

As has already been observed, the power of the rudimentary steam locomotive was strictly limited, and most lines of this period are remarkable for the relatively level routes the engineers were able to create. It was achieved however at some cost, because high embankments, deep cuttings, long viaducts and some stupendous bridges had to be made on most lines to avoid any sharp or lengthy gradients that would have defeated the early locomotives. Brunel and his contemporaries, Robert Stephenson, Joseph Locke, William Cubitt and Charles Vignoles, are often best remembered for the scale and magnificence of the bridge structures they designed to carry their lines across major rivers and estuaries.

The bridges which Brunel created to carry the South Wales Railway across the River Wye at Chepstow, and the Royal Albert Bridge, which took his beloved broad-gauge trains across the River Tamar near Plymouth, must be regarded as his railway engineering masterpieces. He developed an unusual and highly individual form of truss for the main girders. He also pioneered techniques of sinking iron caissons into deep water and sediment to enable secure foundations for the supporting piers to be made on bed-rock, which at both sites was at least eighty feet below the high-water mark of the river.

The proposal to build a railway into Cornwall was first made in 1844, the year the Bristol and Exeter Railway was completed. Brunel had been engineer to this line as he was for the South Devon Railway, the Cornwall and the West Cornwall Railways. He was engaged upon some aspect of the design and construction of these railways for the last fifteen years of his life. In 1844 Brunel believed that a railway bridge across the 1,100-foot-wide River Tamar was out of the question and a steam-powered ferry would be needed to carry rolling stock between Devon and Cornwall. However, it is clear that by the following year when Parliament approved the Cornwall Railway Bill, which allowed for either a ferry at Torpoint or a bridge at Saltash, that Brunel's energies were rising to the challenge; the bridge was sanctioned by Parliament.

Not only was the Tamar a wide and deep river but the proposed route for the line approached it at a great height; insistence by the Admiralty on the usual 100-foot headroom above high-water for sailing vessels com-

The Chepstow railway bridge shortly before it was rebuilt in 1962.
Bristol City Museum and Art Gallery, Woodfin Collection

pounded the difficulties which were indeed awesome. However, the problems to be faced at Chepstow were no less severe; the line from Gloucester to Newport had to cross the River Wye by leaping from near the top of a 120-foot-high sheer cliff on one bank to cross an expanse of loose clay and shingle barely above high water on the other side.

Work commenced first at Saltash in 1847 when some preliminary borings were made using an iron cylinder, six feet in diameter and eighty-five feet long, suspended by secure tackle between two hulks. The top of the cylinder was sealed by iron plates and compressed air was pumped in to create what was, in effect, a massive diving bell. Workmen entered the interior of the cylinder through an air-lock arrangement of double doors; once inside they could work at the bottom of the cylinder, in comparative comfort and safety, excavating the bed of the river and constructing the foundations of the bridge piers. The idea had occurred to Isambard whilst working with his father twenty years before on the Thames Tunnel; it proved to be the key to success at both Saltash and Chepstow.

Using Brunel's iron caisson, 175 trial borings of the bed of the River Tamar were made and by January 1849 a model of the river bed had been made and a short piece of masonry built on the rock some eighty feet below the water to prove the practicability of the proposed design, but the Cornwall Railway Company ran short of money and suspended work for three years. This allowed Brunel, however, to begin work in earnest on the Chepstow bridge, from which he gained valuable experience of sinking the large iron caissons deep into the river bed; air forced in by pumps expelled the water from the bottom of the cylinder allowing workmen to excavate the ground and remove any obstacles which prevented the cylinder sinking under its own weight. Weights were added to force the cylinders down and it was found that some cylinders would sink into place by this means alone; the ground inside other cylinders had to be excavated to get them into position. Once secure, they were filled with concrete to form the foundation of the masonry piers built to support the main trusses of the bridge high above the water.

The main structural element of a bridge is the horizontal girder which spans the distance between the supports of the bridge. The centre of any such girder is deflected down by its own weight and that of the load placed upon it, which in the case of a railway bridge can be relatively massive and sudden. The upper flanges or edges of bridge girders are therefore subjected to enormous compression stresses and if they buckle or deflect sideways, the entire girder may fail. A comprehensive series of experiments and tests, some of them carried out in Bristol in the 1840s, convinced Brunel that cylindrical or oval section tubes fabricated from riveted iron plates were best fitted to withstand the compression stresses to which the upper flanges of bridge girders were subjected. He built a number of smaller bridges including a swing-bridge to carry road traffic across the busy entrance locks leading to Bristol harbour. This

Above: The Royal Albert Bridge a few years after it was completed in 1859.

Bristol City Museum and Art Gallery, Woodfin Collection

Below: The Royal Albert Bridge as it appears today; the road bridge alongside was completed in the 1960s. The scale of Brunel's bridge is still very impressive and its proud inscription above the portals is a fitting tribute to his work.

John Cornwell

The iron swing-bridge Brunel designed to carry road traffic across the south entrance lock of Bristol Harbour is dwarfed by its modern, electrically-powered counterpart – the Plimsoll Bridge – completed in 1964. Brunel's hand-operated bridge was installed in 1848 and subsequently moved to its present location alongside a larger entrance lock opened in 1873. Although no longer in use, the bridge is maintained as a historic feature of Bristol's old dock system.

Paul Elkin

bridge may still be seen, although it is no longer in use; its characteristic tubular section upper flange was a design feature common to them all.

By the time the Chepstow bridge was finished in 1852, he had developed the very characteristic 'Brunel truss' composed of horizontal iron girders on which the platform carrying the rails rested, linked by suspension chains to the ends of a massive circular wrought-iron tube supported fifty feet above the bridge deck on masonry arches through which the trains could pass. Brunel used similar trusses for the Saltash bridge, which is dominated by the twelve foot by sixteen foot oval section upper tube. The Saltash trusses each span 465 feet, some 165 feet longer than those at Chepstow.

Work on the Saltash bridge resumed in 1853 with the construction of the iron caisson cylinder to be used for the main central pier of the bridge – a massive structure in itself, thirty-five feet in diameter at the bottom, with a complex internal arrangement of compartments, connected to the surface through two more cylinders, one inside the other, of six foot and ten foot diameter. The river bed was excavated safely from within the compartments, some delays being caused in 1854 by solid masses of oyster shells, but by February 1855, the cylinder was in place and work started on building the masonry pier.

At the end of 1856, the pier was above water-level and the top section of the iron cylinder was unbolted and removed. Meanwhile the trusses were being fabricated by the side of the river. They weighed over 1,000 tons each, and floating them on iron pontoons out into the river to their positions between the masonry piers was no simple matter. The first truss was launched on 1 September 1857 under Brunel's direction. He insisted on absolute silence from the crowd assembled to watch; he conjured the huge iron construction into position without a hitch, using only flag and whistle signals. Hydraulic jacks were used to raise the truss as masonry was built up underneath; the first span was in place by July 1858.

Brunel was too ill to supervise the placing of the second truss so his assistant, R.P. Brereton, aided by Captain Claxton, undertook the task, which was completed in 1859. A final irony in Brunel's life is that the suspension chains he had made for the Clifton Bridge were purchased by the Cornwall Railway Company and were incorporated into the trusses of the bridge at Saltash. Thus forged from the fires of his youthful enthusiasm at Clifton, the chains were extended for his final triumph at Saltash. The bridge was opened by the Prince Consort in May 1859. Brunel did cross his bridge, but as an invalid on a train. Disease and worry about his last great shipbuilding project, the *Great Eastern*, were killing the great engineer.

THE LAST BATTLE – THE *GREAT EASTERN*

In 1852, Brunel had sketched an idea for an East India steamship, 600 feet long, capable of carrying enough fuel to sail to the southern hemisphere and back without having to refuel. His line of thought was that a ship of such a size, capable of steaming round the world without refuelling, would not only dispense with the expense of establishing and supplying coaling stations, but should prove cheaper to operate than two ships of half the size. It was, however, the relative inefficiency of steam engines and marine boilers at this time that was to undermine this concept.

By the time a contract for the construction of this already enormous vessel was signed in 1853, the length had grown to 693 feet overall, making it twice as long as the *Great Britain*. The tonnage of the vessel, calculated at 27,419 tons, was more than nine times that of the *Great Britain*'s modest 2,984 tons. Brunel thought the new ship would cost half a million pounds. The shipbuilder William Scott Russell tendered a price of £377,200 to build the hull, the two sets of engines, the screw propeller and paddle-wheels. The difference in prices should have excited suspicion, but Brunel was too busy to investigate the discrepancy. It was to cost him his life.

The contract specified that the ship was to be built in a dry-dock, like the *Great Britain*. However, Brunel was persuaded by Scott Russell to build the vessel in his yard at Millwall on the Isle of Dogs and launch the ship *sideways* into the Thames. 1,200 tons of timber were used for piles to support the great weight of the ship and a huge mould-loft (where full-size templates for parts of the ship were made) and a machine-shop, to build the engines, were constructed close by. Work on the ship began in July 1854 and, two and a half years later, the iron-plated timber slipways for launching the vessel were being built.

Money problems, difficulties in getting information from Scott Russell, fires at the yard and the eventual repudiation of the contract by the builder were some of the extra worries that Brunel had to face. Brunel's health began to fail but he was able to restore some sort of order to the project during 1857 and, two months after the floating of the first of the bridge trusses at Saltash, the engineer was in a position to tackle what was, even for him, the unprecedented problem of moving 12,000 tons of ship.

Unfortunately, the quiet expectancy of the crowds in the west was not to be had in London and the orderly system of signals that had worked so well on the Tamar was defeated. The directors of the Eastern Steam Navigation Company, of which Brunel was a major shareholder, had, without telling the engineer, sold over 3,000 tickets admitting the public into the shipyard at Millwall to watch the launch. Although Brunel was prepared for the first attempt to fail, feeling that a stuck ship was better than one moving out of control, much of his careful planning was wasted and in the ensuing chaos, his worst fears were realised.

At first, the ship could not be moved using the arrangement of tackle and giant windlasses provided to haul the vessel down the gently sloping launching ways. However, the use of two large hydraulic rams caused the bow and then the stern to lurch suddenly towards the river, killing an Irish labourer caught by the flailing handle of a huge drum of chain. The *Leviathan*, as the ship had been dubbed, was stuck on the launching ways; the builder Scott Russell, untouched by worry and quite

The *Great Eastern*, photographed by Robert Howlett in November 1857 before her launching.
City of Birmingham Libraries

Captain Harrison, Brunel's chief assistant Jacomb, Brunel and Tredwell, the contractor who built the launching ways, watch anxiously for signs of progress during one of the several attempts made in November 1857 to launch the *Great Eastern*.

Bristol City Museum and Art Gallery

unrepentant about his behaviour, entertained his guests on board in a special gallery in the stern.

Brunel had, on various occasions, offered practical and moral support to fellow engineers like Robert Stephenson when they were in the midst of crucial lifting operations. It was therefore of great value to Brunel, unlike most of the advice given by the public at large, when Stephenson, himself a sick man, came to stand alongside Brunel during his long ordeal when more attempts to launch the ship were made and failed. Almost unbelievable things happened to the machinery; for instance, there was a problem of water being forced through the casing of a stout cast-iron jack like sweat from a human body.

Brunel persevered and was eventually successful, maintaining as he had done on several occasions before, that he would apply more and more force until it was proved that the technique was wrong. Richard Tangye, a Cornishman then just setting up in business in Birmingham to manufacture hydraulic jacks, was called upon to supply ever larger rams, which in the end succeeded in moving the *Great Eastern*, as she was to be called, into the water. Tangye's slogan for years afterwards was: 'We launched the *Great Eastern* and she launched us.'

Eventually, on 31 January 1858, the *Great Eastern* floated on the rising tide and was towed, with Brunel and his family on board, across the river to Deptford for fitting out. She had already cost twice the sum Scott Russell had estimated and was still far from being ready to start earning money at sea. Brunel was, by now, very ill, suffering from chronic inflammation of the kidneys – Bright's disease – named after the physician who was treating him. He travelled with his wife Mary on the Continent, where he still managed to work on his designs for the Eastern Bengal Railway in India. He found on his return home that trade had slumped, so attempts to raise the money to finish the *Great Eastern* had failed.

His doctor insisted Brunel must go to a warm place. He decided on north Africa and had his last Christmas dinner in Cairo in the company of another very sick man, Robert Stephenson. He was able to ascend the rapids above Aswan, an adventure that both he and his son, Henry, enjoyed. Arriving home in May 1859, Brunel found that the directors of a new company which had been formed to finish the *Great Eastern* had ignored his written warning and appointed Scott Russell to fit out the ship. Appalled by the atmosphere of distrust and confusion Scott Russell had again engendered, Brunel took charge and succeeded in getting the ship ready, suffering a stroke four days before she left for Weymouth on her trials.

Making light of heavy seas which sent lesser vessels scurrying for shelter, the great ship passed the Nore Light on 9 September 1859. The ship's massive funnels were surrounded by iron water-jackets which prevented the passenger areas below decks from getting too hot and saved fuel by pre-heating the water fed to the colossal coal-fired boilers. Stop-valves at the top of the water-jackets on the two funnels that passed through the forward passenger saloon, which should have been open, were closed and pressure was building up alarmingly inside the water-jackets. As the ship drew near Hastings, the foremost water-jacket exploded, blowing the funnel into the air in a rush of steam. Six crewmen from the paddle-engine boiler-room were scalded and died horribly soon after the accident, but miraculously, all the passengers had left the saloon and none was hurt. The second valve was opened in time and the ship sailed on.

Paralysed, but still mentally alert at his home in Duke Street in Westminster, Brunel eagerly awaited the account of his ship mastering her element at last. The news of the explosion and the deaths hastened the end of the great man's life. He had risen above disaster again and again; no more. Within six days, Isambard Kingdom Brunel was dead; less than a month later, so too was his friend, Robert Stephenson.

The *Great Eastern* suffered a number of mechanical

Great Eastern at sea; a sight Brunel was never to enjoy. Creating such a massive vessel – it would still be considered a substantial size even today – was a remarkable technical achievement. Its lack of commercial success was due quite simply to the fact that it needed engines of far greater power and efficiency than were available at the time it was built. Many twentieth-century aircraft designs, such as that of the Bristol Brabazon, have suffered a similar fate, and such developments are too often unfairly dismissed as 'white elephants', although in reality technology cannot progress without such pioneering work.

National Maritime Museum

problems during the course of several early voyages carrying passengers across the Atlantic and the cost of repairs forced her owners to sell her in 1862. She was chartered by the Telegraph Construction Company. Her immense size made her the most suitable vessel with which to lay the first trans-oceanic telegraphic cables. The passenger accommodation was removed and replaced by giant cylindrical iron tanks which were capable of holding several thousand miles of underwater cable. The ship was also ideal for cable-laying since she was driven by both paddle-wheels and a screw-propeller; by rotating the paddles and screw in opposite directions, the huge ship could remain still, but under perfect control, in almost any weather. By 27 July 1866, the western end of the first trans-Atlantic telegraph cable was brought ashore from the *Great Eastern*, in Heart's Content Bay, Newfoundland. The giant ship was able to astonish onlookers with her manoeuvrability, pivoting slowly on her centre axis, before steaming majestically out of the narrow inlet to anchor in the bay.

CODA

Brunel achieved so much in his fifty-three years of life, that only by dismissing every item with a line or two, could it all be mentioned in a publication of this size. The authors have endeavoured to give an interesting account of the main elements of his story, but many aspects have had to be left out. These include his marriage and his children; his designs for railways in Italy and in India; his one unsuccessful bridge (over the River Parrett, south of Bridgwater) which was dismantled after only two years and replaced so quietly that hardly anyone noticed; his largely theoretical interest in armaments and his very practical work for the wounded soldiers of the Crimean War.

The books listed on this page, which the authors gratefully acknowledge as the main sources consulted during the preparation of this publication, will enable the interested reader to find out more about the great engineer.

Daniel Gooch, the engineer from Bedlington, near Newcastle-upon-Tyne, who Brunel appointed in 1837 to be the Great Western Railway's first locomotive superintendent and who went on to become its chairman for many years. Referring to Brunel in his memoirs as his 'oldest and best friend', he said that 'the commercial world thought him extravagant, but ... great things are not done by those who sit down and count the cost of every thought and act'.
Bristol City Museum and Art Gallery

Back cover: Modern photograph of Clifton Suspension Bridge.
Paul Elkin

FURTHER READING ABOUT BRUNEL AND HIS WORK

All these publications should be available through your local library which, if it does not have a copy of its own, will be able to borrow one for you through the inter-library loans service. Some of the more recently published titles might also be available from your bookseller.

Beaver, P. *The Big Ship – Brunel's* Great Eastern *– A Pictorial History*, Hugh Evelyn, 1969

Beaver, P. *The Crystal Palace*, Hugh Evelyn, 1970

Body, G. *Clifton Suspension Bridge*, Moonraker Press, 1976

Brunel, I. *The Life of Isambard Kingdom Brunel, Civil Engineer*, first published 1870, reprinted David & Charles, 1971

Buchanan, R.A. & Williams, M. *Brunel's Bristol*, Redcliffe Press, 1982

Corlett, E. *The Iron Ship; the history and significance of Brunel's* Great Britain, Moonraker Press, 1975

Dugan, J. *The Great Iron Ship*, Moonraker Press, 1953

Farr, G. *The Steamship* Great Western, The Historical Association, Bristol Branch, 1963

Farr, G. *The Steamship* Great Britain, The Historical Association, Bristol Branch, 1965

Griffiths, D. *Brunel's* Great Western, Patrick Stephens Ltd, 1985

MacDermot, E.T. *History of the Great Western Railway*, Ian Allan, 1964

Pudney, J. *Brunel and his World*, Thames & Hudson, 1974

Rolt, L.T.C. *Isambard Kingdom Brunel*, Longman, 1957; Penguin, 1970

Thames, R. *Isambard Kingdom Brunel*, Shire Publications, 1972

ISBN 0–7117–0300–0
© 1988 Jarrold Colour Publications
Printed and published in Great Britain by Jarrold Printing, Norwich. 188

ISBN 0-7117-0300-0

9 780711 703001